PICTURES to PARAGRAPHS

WRITING FICTION

Leslie Holleran

Lerner Publications ◆ Minneapolis

Lerner Publications Company
An imprint of Lerner Publishing Group, Inc.
241 First Avenue North
Minneapolis, MN 55401 USA

For reading levels and more information, look up this title at www.lernerbooks.com.

Main body text set in Aptifer Sans LT Pro.
Typeface provided by Linotype AG.

Editor: Angel Kidd **Designer:** Emily Harris **Photo Editor:** Angel Kidd

Library of Congress Cataloging-in-Publication Data

Names: Holleran, Leslie author
Title: Writing fiction / Leslie Holleran.
Description: Minneapolis : Lerner Publications, 2026. | Series: Pictures to paragraphs | Includes bibliographical references and index. | Audience: Ages 8–12 | Audience: Grades 4–6 | Summary: "Fiction can take many forms from fantastical to historical, but what are the main components? This guide uses photo prompts to spark readers' imaginations and guide them through the process of writing a fictional piece"— Provided by publisher.
Identifiers: LCCN 2025015095 (print) | LCCN 2025015096 (ebook) | ISBN 9798765688809 library binding | ISBN 9798348028794 paperback | ISBN 9798765695944 epub
Subjects: LCSH: Fiction—Authorship—Juvenile literature
Classification: LCC PN3355 .H65 2026 (print) | LCC PN3355 (ebook) | DDC 808.3—dc23/eng/20250414

LC record available at https://lccn.loc.gov/2025015095
LC ebook record available at https://lccn.loc.gov/2025015096

Manufactured in the United States of America
1-1012675-54710-7/2/2025

TABLE OF CONTENTS

CRAFTING A STORY

The queen slipped out of bed and into her coat. She walked quickly through empty hallways to the castle entrance. *Who could be knocking at this hour?* she wondered. She opened the door and gasped.

This is an example of fiction. Fiction is a made-up story that has not happened in real life. In nonfiction, the people, places, and events are real and based on verifiable facts. When writing fiction, it helps to think about and develop a story's characters and plot before diving in. That's the first stage of the writing process—planning. Then you'll write a draft based on your plan.

In the second stage, you'll share your draft with peers. After getting feedback, you'll evaluate the suggestions and revise your work. The third and final stage involves editing the revised draft and then publishing it. The photos and writing prompts in this book aim to spark your imagination and help you write great fictional stories. Let's get started!

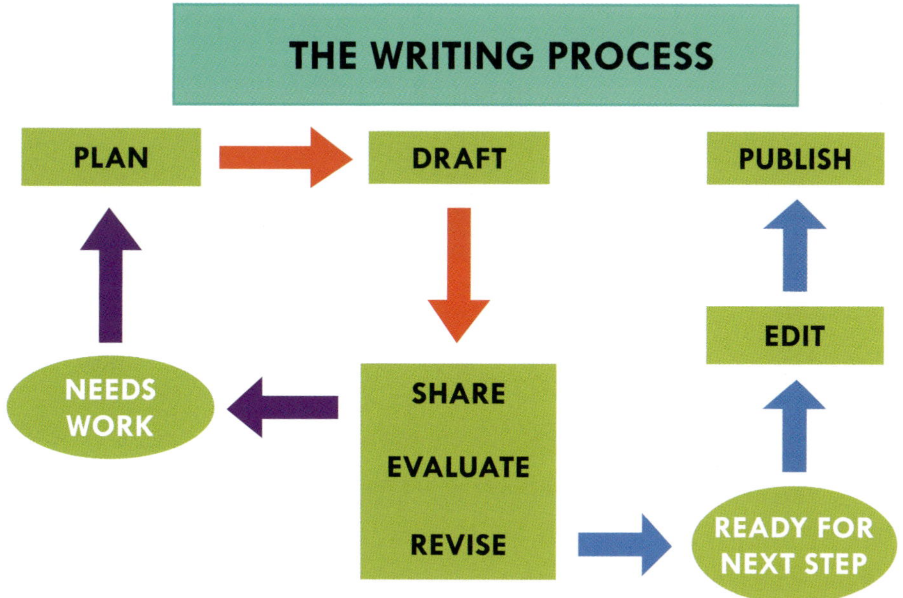

CHAPTER 1
CREATING CHARACTERS

One of the most exciting parts of writing fiction is creating characters from scratch. Characters are essential to fiction. There is no story without one or more of them. The writer's job is to develop interesting characters in relation to one another.

The main character is the central figure. Secondary characters have different roles to play in the main character's development. Characters become believable as details about them are revealed. For example, in a story about a doctor, readers may learn that his sister has had an incurable condition since birth. Her ongoing treatment motivated him to become a doctor to help people like her. The doctor is the main character, and his sister is a secondary character.

Characters should say and do things real people would say and do.

When characters are well developed in a short story or novel, readers get to know a lot about them. In a shorter work, there's only room for key details. But no matter the length of the story, the main character should always develop, or change, based on the events that have happened.

WRITING PROMPT: CHARACTER DESCRIPTIONS

Create a character who is a scientist. Invent a name for her. What was she like as a child and teen? What were her favorite and least favorite subjects in school? Why did she want to become a scientist? What has she achieved or discovered in her work?

Point of view (POV) determines who's telling the story and what information readers learn about the characters. There are three main points of view—first, second, and third person. The use of pronouns such as *I*, *me*, and *mine* signal that the first person POV is being used. If you keep a diary or journal, you're writing in first person. Everything is written in your POV.

WRITING PROMPT: FIRST PERSON POV

You get to tell the story of this sleepover. Write in first person as if you're the girl jumping on the bed. Imagine it is the best sleepover ever. What happens? Use your imagination!

The use of the pronouns you, your, and yours indicate second person POV. With this POV, the reader is the one intended to perform the action. It is often used in how-to guides. Third person is the most frequently used POV in fiction. Some pronouns that give away this POV are *he*, *she*, *they*, *his*, *hers*, and *theirs*. Third person can be beneficial for fiction writers because it offers the most flexibility. It allows a writer to move between characters and share different perspectives rather than being confined to just one perspective.

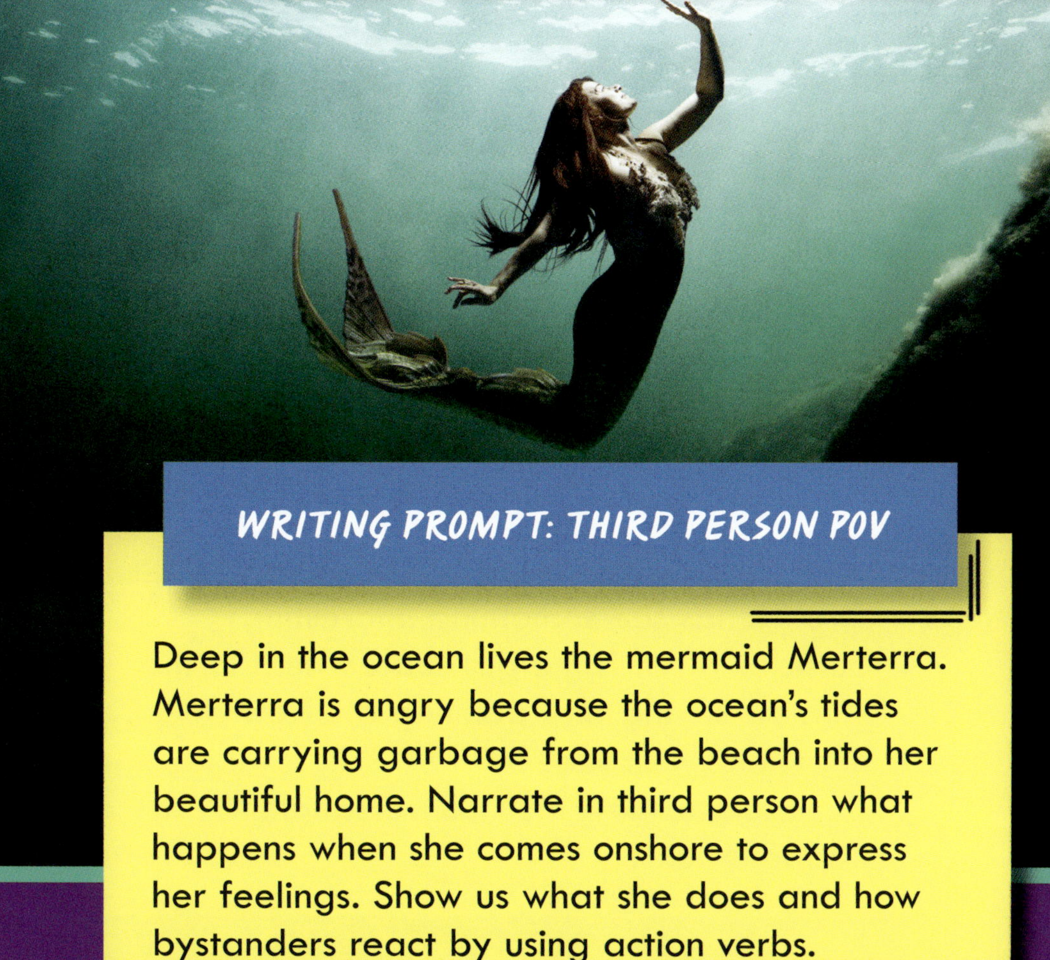

WRITING PROMPT: THIRD PERSON POV

Deep in the ocean lives the mermaid Merterra. Merterra is angry because the ocean's tides are carrying garbage from the beach into her beautiful home. Narrate in third person what happens when she comes onshore to express her feelings. Show us what she does and how bystanders react by using action verbs.

Dialogue lets readers hear from characters directly. Through dialogue, an author can reveal how characters are feeling, what they want and need, and what their relationships are with other characters. Dialogue can also help move the plot forward.

Imagine a conversation between two friends playing a sport. What would they say to each other if one of them got hurt? The conversation might go like this:

Leo ran over to the goal. "What happened, Liv?" he asked.

"I hit my knee. It hurts!" she cried. "Can you get Coach?"

"I'll be right back," Leo said. He sprinted down the field toward the coach.

WRITING PROMPT: DIALOGUE

Two friends see something interesting outside. What is the girl seated next to the window saying and pointing at? How does her friend respond? Write a scene with dialogue to show their conversation. What happens next?

CHAPTER 2

HOW A STORY UNFOLDS

Plot is a sequence of events that holds a story together. There are all kinds of stories, from adventures and quests to comedies and tragedies. Characters drive the plot forward.

In quests and adventures, the main character pursues an important goal, sometimes with the help of secondary characters. Or another character might work in opposition to the main character, trying to prevent them from getting what they want.

All characters have a goal, whether it is big or small.

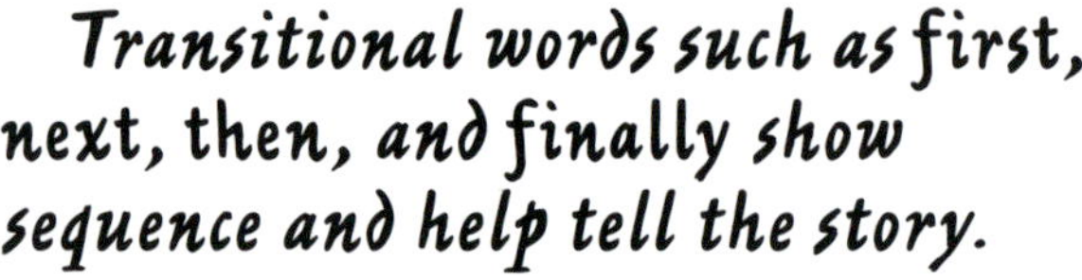

Transitional words such as* first, next, then, *and* finally *show sequence and help tell the story.

Other words such as *because* and *since* show cause and effect. Here's an example using both types of transitional words:

Austin won an award! Then he tripped on the way to the podium to get his trophy because he didn't look where he was going. Next, he smiled broadly. Since he was a winner, he wasn't going to let a little embarrassment steal his joy.

WRITING PROMPT: TRANSITIONS

You and a friend are making cupcakes. All the ingredients are in the kitchen. What happens from start to finish? Write a believable sequence from baking to frosting using transitional words.

Many stories begin by introducing the main character and describing a problem the character is facing. Here's an example: LJ desperately wanted a dog. She longed to stroke soft puppy fur and get nibbled by sharp puppy teeth. LJ had a big case of one-sided puppy love.

The middle of a story focuses on the actions the main character takes to solve their problem. The middle is generally the longest part of the story. In LJ's case, she needed her parents' permission before she could get a dog. So, she had to prove she could take care of one. The middle could describe what she did to prove she was capable. To create rising action, her efforts became bigger and bigger until her parents made up their minds.

A story's ending provides a conclusion to the original problem. For LJ there was a happy ending. Her parents got her a puppy!

WRITING PROMPT: SEQUENCE OF EVENTS

Oh no, Harvey got out again! Narrate a fast-paced story about this lost dog named Harvey, where he goes, and how his family finds him. Keep your sentences short to help the action move quickly.

LOST DOG
Friendly, white with one brown spot.
Answers to Harvey. Call 744-555-0129.
REWARD if found and returned.
744-555-0129
744-555-0129
744-555-0129
744-555-0129
744-555-0129
744-555-0129
744-555-0129
744-555-0129
744-555-0129

CHAPTER 3

WHERE AND WHEN

You can bring a setting to life with sensory details.

These details rely on your senses of sight, sound, smell, touch, and taste. Here's a short, sensory description of this beach scene:

The children were thrilled to go to the beach with their parents that evening. It had been another hot day, and everyone needed to cool off. The kids raced to the water, the sand squishing beneath their feet. Salty sea spray flew everywhere as all five children charged into the surf. The ocean never felt better!

WRITING PROMPT: SENSORY DETAILS

Bring this campfire scene to life with sensory details. What does the fire sound like? What does the smoke smell like? How do the marshmallows taste? Include a variety of details to transport the reader into the scene.

Sometimes a story's setting is very specific. The location is important, but *when* the events take place also has significance. For example, many stories revolve around holidays such as Valentine's Day or Halloween. Certain events and activities occur on holidays—these can be woven into the plot. Additionally, the time of day and season of the year could be significant to a story. It's also possible to make a giant leap in time when writing fiction. A story could be set in the past or one hundred years into the future.

WRITING PROMPT: SETTING

While out trick-or-treating at dusk on Halloween, you and your friends come upon what looks like a haunted house. Describe the house and its surroundings in detail. What sounds do you hear? Are there any odors? What is the temperature, and how do the characters feel about it?

CHAPTER 4

REVISE AND SHINE

It's a great idea to get feedback on your story from other readers and writers. A peer may have an idea to take your plot to the next level that you had never thought of, or they might catch typos and grammar mistakes you missed. After you've considered all the feedback, it's time to revise. All writers revise their work, from beginners to professionals. No one gets it exactly right the first time.

In the next prompt, you will revisit your haunted house description and add onto it. Your description of the setting becomes the beginning of a spooky Halloween tale. When you're done, share your story and then revise.

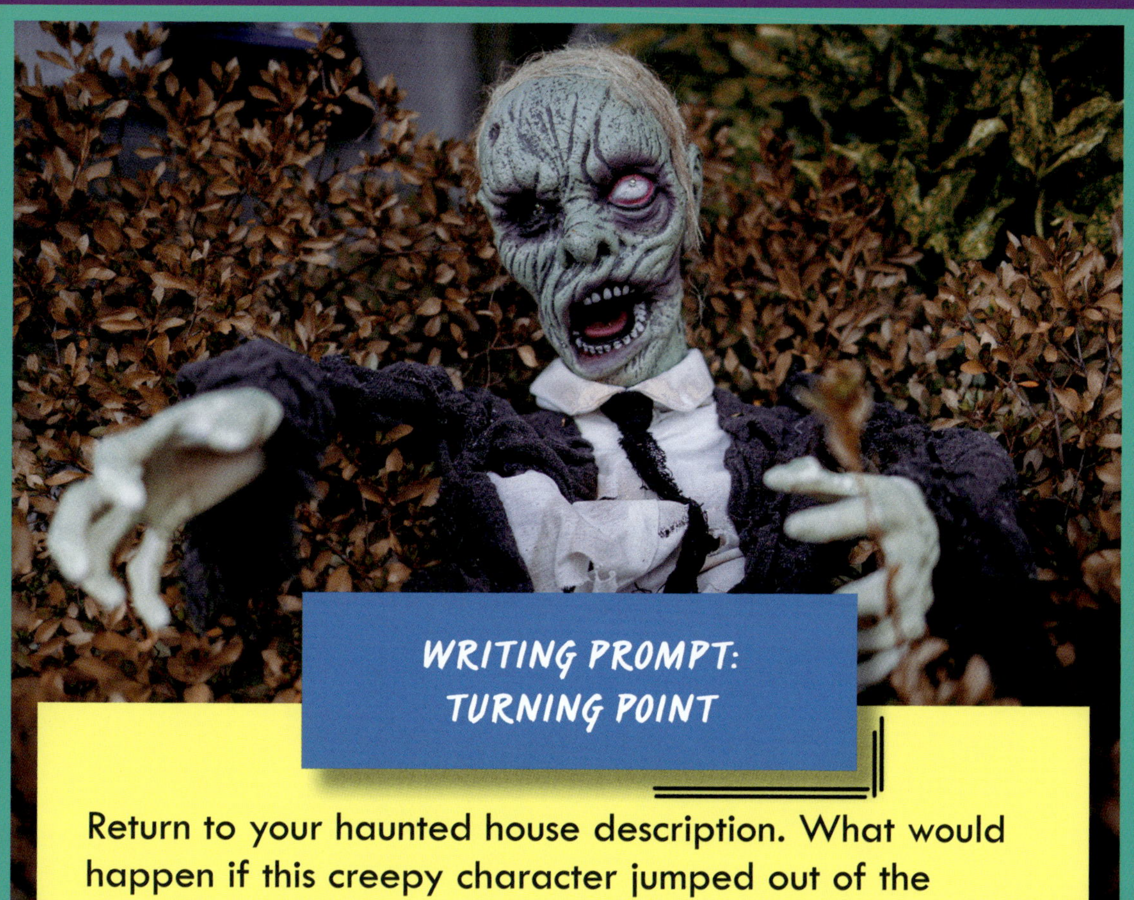

WRITING PROMPT: TURNING POINT

Return to your haunted house description. What would happen if this creepy character jumped out of the bushes as you approached the front door? Use this turn of events in the plot to create rising action. Don't forget to describe the character. What happens next? How does the story end?

Even natural processes have stories that can be used as the basis for fiction. Consider the life cycle of a caterpillar. This insect starts out as an egg, then develops into a chrysalis, and finally emerges as a butterfly. There's a very clear sequence of events and an exciting climax. The sequence repeats itself all over when the butterfly lays eggs.

WRITING PROMPT: FULL CIRCLE ENDINGS

Create a story based on the caterpillar life cycle. Since this is a fictional story, you can give your caterpillar character feelings and emotions. Be sure to include each stage of their life, creating a clear sequence of events. Again, share your story to get feedback, then revise.

Storytelling magic can only happen if you put your pen to paper or hands on the keyboard. Let your words flow from your brain to the page. Editing and revisions come later. In learning the craft of writing, no matter what kind, you'll benefit from reading. If you want to write science fiction that's out of this world, then read that kind of fiction for inspiration. Someone else's work may give you ideas.

Like any other skill, writing great stories takes a lot of practice. Rest assured that the more you write, the better you'll get. Just give yourself a chance and try.

GLOSSARY

action verb: a word that describes a person or thing performing an action

character: a person, animal, or being in a story that is crucial to the plot

climax: the most important and exciting part of a story

dialogue: conversation between two or more characters

draft: a written version of a story

narrate: to tell a story in detail

nonfiction: a story that is not invented but based on facts

plot: the events that move a story along

point of view (POV): the perspective or view of the narrator

rising action: the events that follow the beginning of a story and lead to the climax

setting: where and when a story takes place

LEARN MORE

BBC Bitesize: Different Kinds of Texts—Fiction and Nonfiction
https://www.bbc.co.uk/bitesize/articles/z6yq96f

Brittanica Kids: Fiction
https://kids.britannica.com/kids/article/fiction/400074

Eason, Sarah, and Louise Spilsbury. *How Do I Write Well?* Cheriton Children's Books, 2022.

Kiddle: Fiction Facts for Kids
https://kids.kiddle.co/Fiction

Mrs. Wordsmith. *How to Write a Story*. DK, 2022.

Ood, Ollie. *How to Write a Novel Before You Turn 13*. Calamari Tales, 2021

Schwartz. Heather E. *Writing Drama*. Lerner Publications, 2026.

Twinkl: Fiction
https://www.twinkl.com/teaching-wiki/fiction

INDEX

PHOTO ACKNOWLEDGMENTS

Image credits: Kharchenko_irina7/Getty Images, p. 4; Klaus Vedfelt/Getty Images, p. 6; Solskin/Getty Images, p. 7; AaronAmat/Getty Images, p. 9; Willie B. Thomas/Getty Images, p. 10; Henrik Sorensen/Getty Images, p. 11; Estradaanton/Getty Images, p. 13; DianaHirsch/Getty Images, p. 14; Vladimir Vladimirov/Getty Images, p. 15; Morsa Images/Getty Images, p. 17; Jeffrey Coolidge/Getty Images, p. 19; Peter Cade/Getty Images, p. 20; Yana Iskayeva/Getty Images, p. 21; Mint Images/Getty Images, p. 23; kali9/Getty Images, p. 24; OsakaWayne Studios/Getty Images, p. 25; catchlights_sg/Getty Images, p. 27; Sean Anthony Eddy/Getty Images, p. 29. Design elements: Olex Runda/Shutterstock; Claudio Divizia/Shutterstock.

Cover: Ed Freeman/Getty Images.